*where did it all go wrong?*

*written by rayaan*

*where did it all go wrong?*

i gave you the world,
and you gave me the moon,
but we weren't meant to be.

*where did it all go wrong?*

the scars you left,
will never heal,
and it's hard to accept,
the damage you left behind.

*where did it all go wrong?*

you took my breath away,
and left me breathless,
with nothing left to breathe,
you left me when i thought,
you'd keep me breathing forever.

*where did it all go wrong?*

**is it my fault?**
do you blame me for the pain?
or is it an excuse for always letting it rain?
you left me with excess baggage.
you made me feel like a savage.
you dealt cards that cause damage.
and now this ocean is hard to manage.
you didn't bother to explain.
you made up excuses for the stains.
and now i'm expected to forgive.
when you took everything i had to give.

*where did it all go wrong?*

was i ever enough or,
was it always someone else?
did i just help you leave?
or did i bring it upon myself,
to grieve losing you?

*where did it all go wrong?*

i've missed you,
since the moment you left,
and i haven't been able to,
fill the void that you created.

*where did it all go wrong?*

i can never get over you,
because the tears that i've shed,
could fill oceans upon oceans,
flooding every land on this planet.

*where did it all go wrong?*

**unbelievable**
will i ever heal? are we really over? is this actually real? you taught me how to enjoy this life. but i can't enjoy it without you. now, i need to learn how to survive without you. but you don't know how hard it is to deal with this world by myself. i'm suffering in silence and you don't have a clue. you painted my world brightly and then repainted it dark blue. i'm working harder to paint a new world without you in it. because i deserve to be content with just myself. and i should be able accept that you're no longer a part of my world. and one day, i'll be able to stay afloat and find myself back ashore.

*where did it all go wrong?*

my fears came true,
you disappeared,
and i can't fathom,
how easy it was,
for you to walk away.

*where did it all go wrong?*

i didn't forget you,
but i know you forgot me,
as if our love disappeared overnight.

*where did it all go wrong?*

### *bridges*
we burnt bridges because everything ended on a sour note. and the feelings we felt weren't left in anything we wrote. i think we broke each other's hearts. we always thought we would last. we had the wrong expectations. maybe we had the wrong connection. and that was apparent upon further reflection. the mirrors deceived our minds. because we walked into this room hoping there was something else to find. i don't think our paths were ever meant to cross. because we forced an idea that we previously lost.

*where did it all go wrong?*

i didn't think you'd hurt me,
i never thought it'd cause pain,
but you could argue the same,
it was just a shame,
that our perspectives differed.

*where did it all go wrong?*

i sacrificed my world for you,
i gave up my life and my feelings,
just to accommodate your love,
but none of that was enough,
now i'm in need of the heaviest healing,
because you've taken off,
with parts of me that i can't recover,
and a chunk of my life,
that will never be the same.

*where did it all go wrong?*

### *locksmith*
you were the locksmith to my heart, but then you became heartless. a natural disaster that erupted out of thin air. so, i question why did we start this? was this fair for the both of us? locking my heart and throwing away the key was unjust. but it was my fault for giving you access to the best parts of me. i gave you my heart to take shelter in. little did i know, you would just be guest instead of a permanent resident. and now i'm left to pick up the remnants that you scattered across the world.

*where did it all go wrong?*

our souls met so long ago,
but we weren't meant to be,
more than just friends,
just guests passing by,
for a temporary amount of time.

*where did it all go wrong?*

is there still,
something there between us?
or did everything disappear,
before you left?

*where did it all go wrong?*

our love was one,
that money couldn't buy,
that's why it hurts,
so much more losing it.

*where did it all go wrong?*

**invest**
i gave you memories. i gave you all of my energy. i wish it could have lasted longer. because you made my heart stronger. i wish you could have been happier with my company. because i only ever loved you abundantly. now i've been abandoned with my heart in two pieces. and every other object reminds me of you, so my heart freezes. how do i move on after investing my heart and soul into you? how do i fill in the holes that you left?

*where did it all go wrong?*

it hurts knowing that,
you'll be moving on,
with someone else,
moving on with someone,
that isn't me,
doing all of the things,
we used to do together,
loving and laughing,
the way we did before,
everything came crashing down,
living the life,
we were supposed to live.

*where did it all go wrong?*

### *used to you*
i'm used to you. i'm used to the late nights and brunch dates. but i got the memo too late. i'm used to the dining and dancing. i'm used to the sunny strolls through the city. i'm used to the texts telling me that you miss me. i'm used to the star gazing we'd do every summer. in this black and white world, you added so much colour. now i have find solitude in my own company. i play the songs you like to remember the good times, and every time the tears trickle down my face. i feel so out place because i'm so used to having you in my space. i got so used to you, now i have to get used to losing you. i wish i didn't grow so attached to something so temporary.

*where did it all go wrong?*

### *give up*
did you give up because things got too hard? or did you give up because i was never written on your cards? i tried to take care of us, but you stopped trying. and it's my fault for never noticing when the flowers start dying. did we come to a natural end? were we just better off as friends? friends that stop speaking because the love faded away. maybe i'm naïve for thinking that your love would always stay. i wish we could start again, maybe we could have done things differently. or maybe you could have let me down gently. next time, heal me before you leave me. and tell me our expiration date before you deceive me.

*where did it all go wrong?*

we went from life partners,
to strangers,
in what feels like,
the quickest decision.

*where did it all go wrong?*

if we met again as strangers,
would you love me all over again?
or would you know better,
than to waste your time on me?

*where did it all go wrong?*

you had my heart,
you had my mind,
you had my soul,
you had my loyalty,
and i treated you like royalty,
i gave you every part of me,
i hope you find all of these things,
with someone other than me.

*where did it all go wrong?*

**why?**
you hurt me in ways that i can never recover. why did you love me if you were going to make me suffer? you left my heart in pieces. you did the opposite of helping me find peace. i gave you a sanctity and you gave me hell. now i'm staring at your ghost inside of a mental cell. why did you engage with me if you didn't want it to last? because you're not a part of a tainted past. a memory that turned into a nightmare. and i thought finding you was rare. so, i question my judgement. and any ounce of hope becomes redundant. so, i hide every issue. discard tissue after tissue. hoping the well will run dry. because every wish i make becomes a pointless lie.

*where did it all go wrong?*

i wish i could hurt you,
the way you hurt me,
so, i could teach you,
what it means to suffer,
from the hardest pain,
the incurable heartbreak.

*where did it all go wrong?*

who hurt you,
for you to hurt me like this?
did we deserve these,
twisted turns?
did we need to watch,
our bridges burn?

*where did it all go wrong?*

i thought people didn't change,
but you did and so did i,
and we drifted further apart,
separately lost at sea,
stranded on different islands,
leading and living new lives,
it was as if we never existed,
within each other's memories.

*where did it all go wrong?*

### *relief*
you were my relief. but you only gave me deceit. i've been through this before. i've tackled war. i've walked into a thousand swords before. i didn't expect this pain to repeat. i didn't think this pain would make me feel incomplete. i feel like i put these burdens on myself. because i ignored everyone's help. i've accepted that i deserve this. so i spend hours searching for light in the abyss. i avoid the difficult scars by closing my eyes. every demon that finds me multiplies. so whilst i run away i try to complete this puzzle. but missing pieces and constant pressures are difficult to juggle. i blame myself for being young. and for failing to realise when i was stung.

*where did it all go wrong?*

our souls weren't meant to be soulmates,
just lessons on how to love,
but losing you wasn't enough,
because i only learnt,
what love isn't supposed to be.

*where did it all go wrong?*

maybe we both didn't deserve better,
maybe we just deserve different things.

*where did it all go wrong?*

i gave you the real me,
because i thought you were special.

*where did it all go wrong?*

### *affection*
i gave you the sweetest and dearest love. tell me why it wasn't enough. i wiped away every single tear. i fought every single fear. tell me why you fell out of love. tell me that my love wasn't enough. because i gave you more than just affection. i gave you the deepest connection. guiding you through every trial and tribulation. being at your side in every situation. loyal to the core. opening every single door. a gentleman at every corner of our lives. a partner and best friend in every drive. tell me why i feel so betrayed. i made a mistake leaving my heart and soul displayed. tell me why i should have kept my heart on my sleeves. because i never thought you'd be someone i'd have to grieve.

*where did it all go wrong?*

it was us against the world,
until we decided,
to fight our struggles alone,
it's so much harder without you,
and i hope you feel the same way.

*where did it all go wrong?*

i thought the future would be you and i,
but it looks like it's going to be,
just me, myself and i,
and you'll be recreating our story,
with someone other than me.

*where did it all go wrong?*

### *leaves*
you said you'd stay forever but that was just a lie. maybe it's my fault for allowing myself to believe in your lie. is it a crime to put your full trust in the words of someone you trust? because i lived as if nothing could stop us. the only thing that could destroy our world was each other. and you found a way to make us suffer. forever was a pipe dream because everything comes to an end. even the leaves eventually descend.

*where did it all go wrong?*

whenever i stare into the sky,
i see an empty blanket of darkness,
you were the star in my life,
the glimmer of hope that kept me going,
but it faded away far too soon.

*where did it all go wrong?*

**broken crown**
i still see you in my dreams, but you're also the reason i can't sleep. my eyes run dry even though you've made me weep. i remember every time you held onto my hand and when you finally let go. i was so happy to meet you but now i regret that i met you. you were the solution to my world but also the worst mistake. you put my heart together again just for it to break. stabilising my smile just to flip my world upside down. but i still have dreams of giving you a crown.

*where did it all go wrong?*

the mirror i stare into is broken,
pieces are missing,
so every reflection is incomplete,
my soul has been left wide open,
now it feels like part of me isn't living,
i wish this was an episode i could delete.

*where did it all go wrong?*

maybe i can't forgive you,
because i still miss you.

*where did it all go wrong?*

our paths might be broken,
but i hoped they'd cross again.

*where did it all go wrong?*

i wish you the best,
and without me,
i hope your heart can rest,
because you were,
never content,
but i won't ever resent you,
even though we didn't last,
we just weren't a match,
so i wish you the best.

*where did it all go wrong?*

**a letter to the future you**
are you happy with all your choices? because it took me a while to get rid of your voice. i was lucky to get out of everything alive. but did you manage to survive? do you still see me beside you in the mirror or have you stopped reflecting? i wish i knew that we were on the verge of disconnecting. maybe it would have hurt less. but i know now that i didn't deserve this. so is the cup half empty now that i've been erased? is the mural of me in your heart defaced? now that your environment is different, has anything changed? i have all these questions now that we're estranged. i don't want you to regret me. but i also don't want you to forget me. i want you to know i'm doing better in a world where i had to unlearn your love. i experienced growth in understanding that love isn't always enough. so i hope when you were looking for the next one, you were still kind. or when you searched for the next victim, you had me in mind?

*where did it all go wrong?*

i tried to be there for you,
in your hardest times,
i just wish you could,
reciprocate my efforts,
was it so wrong,
to have any expectations?

*where did it all go wrong?*

it didn't work out,
the way we thought it would,
but i guess it was,
for our own good.

*where did it all go wrong?*

i gave you my soul,
because you were,
the love of my life,
but you returned it,
with a blackhole.

*where did it all go wrong?*

souls depart regularly,
but i didn't expect,
for your soul to let go of mine,
you made it so hard,
to trust another soul again.

*where did it all go wrong?*

i cry when i think of you,
because you were,
the love of my life,
and you broke every part of me,
i lie when i say i don't think of you,
because you were,
the life severing knife,
that shred my heart to pieces.

*where did it all go wrong?*

**was it real?**
was any of this love real? the smiles and the hugs. was it a mistake to give you my heart to steal? i guess my complete commitment wasn't enough. loving you didn't do me any favours. it just extinguished my soft nature. it's hard to believe in trust. when breaking my heart feels so unjust. healing feels so farfetched so it feels like nothing can save me. and now i've fallen so far down into a pit where everyone will hate me. i've got nowhere left to hide from the memories of us. because i'm living in a cemetery of what we once were.

*where did it all go wrong?*

you left without an explanation,
so where do i find closure?
because without you,
i'm nowhere closer.

*where did it all go wrong?*

i wanted you to stay,
because now i miss you every day,
but you were never worth the tears,
crying over my biggest fears coming true,
my biggest waste of time was you,
if i could erase our history,
i would make sure you remained as a mystery.

*where did it all go wrong?*

**switch**
if we could switch lives, would you be okay with me hurting you? you'd probably make a scene, telling everyone i'm not deserving of you. so why did you think it was okay to destroy the flowers i gave you? did you waste all my hours so that i could hate you? i preferred the sunshine in my life but you brought every grey cloud. bringing torrential rain and ounces of doubt. breaking the vase every time glued the pieces back together again. it felt like everything you did was driving me insane.

*where did it all go wrong?*

i feel so blue,
when i think of you,
my soul is hurting more than i show you,
now i wish i didn't know you,
but you taught me lessons,
lessons in love that gave me progression,
so when i think of you,
even though it hurts,
i guess i'll always love you.

*where did it all go wrong?*

maybe i love you more,
now that you're not there,
maybe i love you more,
now that you don't care.

*where did it all go wrong?*

**_forever_**
i said i'd love you forever. but that stopped when we were no longer together. i would have carried on loving you the way you wanted to be loved. but i felt nothing from you when we last hugged. i knew it was over but you didn't need to give me empty reasons. if only i knew your heart would change like the seasons. you took me on a rollercoaster of emotions. leaving me to drown in the ocean. i thought we were unstoppable. but in your eyes, i was always droppable. i said i'd love you until the end of time. but i didn't think i would be the victim of your biggest crime.

*where did it all go wrong?*

i gave you my heart,
and the best parts of me,
i gave you my soul and my mind,
and the love you were hoping to find,
your name still rolls off my tongue,
and your voice echoes around me,
i wish i could have given you my eyes,
so you could see yourself without any lies,
i helped you grow wings,
elevating you so your heart could sing,
and i no longer have the privilege,
of enjoying your company.

*where did it all go wrong?*

if you ever change your mind,
maybe i'll be waiting for you,
but i won't be in the place you left me,
i'll be on the other side,
living the dreams that were meant for us,
finding myself after trauma made me hide,
no longer hating myself for losing us,
accepting that i was better off without you.

*where did it all go wrong?*

did we bid farewell too soon?
or did we waste too much time?

*where did it all go wrong?*

**over you**
i'm trying to get over you, but everything reminds me of you. there's no leaving you behind. because you always find a way back inside my mind. i can't be happy without remembering i'm not enjoying this happiness with you. you're still living in the corners of my mind. every time i try to heal, you're the only thing i can find. your touch is still over this house. your soul still taunts me in the middle of night so i silently shout. the bedsheets still smell of your favourite fragrance. and it hurts that now i'm just a former acquaintance.

*where did it all go wrong?*

i don't think i can ever love again,
because i don't want to go through,
this pain all over again.

*where did it all go wrong?*

you told me not to worry,
and that you wouldn't leave,
but i didn't read the fine print,
so i only have myself to blame.

*where did it all go wrong?*

**deserving**
i didn't deserve you, and you didn't deserve me. i know that i hurt you, but you also hurt me. we didn't take accountability for the broken glass. we didn't try to sow new seeds for greener grass. we messed up the puzzle by losing the pieces. we put our own heart outside, watching how it freezes. destroying the beautiful flower that we grew. and purposely reconstructing the home we broke with glue. we didn't try hard enough to save us. or maybe that was just you, or maybe that was me, but it's easier to say, us.

*where did it all go wrong?*

i still blame myself,
for what we could have been,
for what we would have been,
i feel helpless,
because it's all my fault.

*where did it all go wrong?*

it's so hard to explain,
that i'm in love with the idea,
of what you once meant to me,
and now that idea only lives,
inside of my dismantled mind.

*where did it all go wrong?*

### *archived*
i couldn't breathe without you, i would be overwhelmed by anxiety. but you always made me your priority. you took my breath away when you left. so i had no saviour to intercept. without you i've had to learn how to survive on my own. and now i've decided i'm better off alone. i never should have depended on you to survive. i had to come back up without you when i took that dive. i almost didn't lift this anvil off my shoulders. now i need to forget you, so i've thrown you into the deepest folder.

*where did it all go wrong?*

**regret**
i feel sorry for you, because i loved you more than anyone else could. but i didn't know that love wasn't good. i tried to be your hero during your toughest times. when i judge myself, that was my biggest crime. because i gave myself to someone who didn't give themselves back. i was willing to lay myself on the track. just so you could be content with your reality. but looking back, it was pure insanity. i loved you hard and that's why it hurt so much to lose you. and that's also why i wish i didn't choose you.

*where did it all go wrong?*

you were the fire,
that kept my wind burning,
but you decided to take,
all of my energy away,
and put out the flames,
so everything to do with us,
could die a sorrowful death.

*where did it all go wrong?*

after you left,
it felt like death,
it was temporary,
but it felt like a lifetime,
because i'm mourning,
the memories we once had,
and the future we planned.

*where did it all go wrong?*

### **wandering**
i know you've already left, but i don't know how to leave. i'm still figuring out how to breathe. even though the home we made is empty. i can't change that you've already left me. i'll resent you for a little longer. whilst i figure out how to get stronger. because i never planned for a world without you. so i'm reliving every moment without you. it's so hard to leave the home we made. i'm wandering around each corridor hoping the memories would fade. every room reminds me of the warmth and comfort. and how each room had a love that was abundant. do you miss it the way i do? or am i the only one that's missing you?

*where did it all go wrong?*

### ghost
your ghost still follows me with every memory. there's no letting go of your energy. when the rain falls i remember every tear dropped. and every night i relive when my heart stopped. i lay in a bed that was meant for us. reminiscing how you abandoned us. in every corner of the world, i can't get rid of you from my mind. i wish i could forget the person you once were. but i always find a way for everything to hurt.

*where did it all go wrong?*

you were the lesson i needed,
so that i could be content with solitude,
we let the ink bleed,
watering the seed,
so the petals could blossom,
and wither away one by one.

*where did it all go wrong?*

it's a lonely life alone,
i find myself revisiting memories on my own,
now there's nothing left of you,
so i'm stuck missing the ghost of you.

*where did it all go wrong?*

i'm a hopeless romantic,
compensating for being loveless,
so if my love was too strong,
you could have told me where i was wrong,
instead, you didn't tell me you got tired,
and set my heart on fire.

*where did it all go wrong?*

i'll always love you,
even though you stopped loving me.

*where did it all go wrong?*

we used to be close,
essentially inseparable,
but our curtains closed,
even though the show was memorable,
early mornings and late nights,
turned into mourning and story highlights,
i wish this chapter ended slower,
but nothing could change,
that it would eventually be over.

*where did it all go wrong?*

**because of you**

you're the reason i don't want to love anymore. you ripped out everything and left my guts on the floor. now i only associate love with pain. so do i have the right to say you drove me insane? i let myself be vulnerable around you. i made sure only light and positivity would surround you. in return you left me in a vacuum, trapped forever. i wouldn't have minded if you didn't promise that we'd do everything together.

*where did it all go wrong?*

it's probably best,
that we go our separate ways,
because never really matched,
our souls fought against each other,
instead of in unison.

*where did it all go wrong?*

instead of being,
fire and water,
we were fire and wind,
growing a flame,
that we could never contain.

*where did it all go wrong?*

i'm still putting out the fire,
that you left me inside of,
i'm trying not to resent you,
but i'm tired of hurting over you.

*where did it all go wrong?*

### *helping hand*
i helped you hurt me by loving you too hard. you warned me when i picked up the cards in my hand. i didn't listen and i can't just blame you for the mess. the emotions ran wild so the chaos would never rest. you threw me under the bus. you pushed me off of the cliff when i gave you, my trust. you gave me the rope to climb back up and let go whilst i was halfway. opening the door for me step inside when you were never going to stay. creating memories just to turn them into nightmares. abandoning me when you promised to rescue me from despair. loving me just to leave. ending everything about us just so i could grieve.

*where did it all go wrong?*

the thought of losing you,
hurt so much more,
when it became true.

*where did it all go wrong?*

everywhere i turn,
i'm looking for closure,
every bridge is burnt,
and every path is over,
there's no escaping,
the pain of losing my other half,
how will i ever feel again,
because i'm too numb to ever heal again.

*where did it all go wrong?*

### *nights*
these late nights will never be the same because i spend them alone. contemplating what it feels like from going from you to on my own. the other side of the bed is permanently vacant. i lie next to it, i'm so hopelessly patient. you're never going to return that's why the windowsill is gathering dust. and i wouldn't let you in again because you broke my trust. the curtains are staying closed until i'm ready to let the light back in. the stars aren't the same so i don't think i'll let the night back in. your scent still linger in my mind, it's hard to erase. and every night when i close my eyes i still see your face.

*where did it all go wrong?*

this love stopped working,
and it started hurting,
we deserved more than just pain,
but we left these permanent stains,
was any of this worth it,
did either of us deserve it,
did we call it quits too soon,
or did we dream too much looking at the moon?

*where did it all go wrong?*

maybe i shouldn't have rushed,
because you weren't the person for me,
even though it hurt a lot,
it gave me the lessons i needed to grow.

*where did it all go wrong?*

i still carry all the blame,
maybe we were just playing games,
but we didn't share the responsibility,
for burning down the castle we built,
we let the walls crumble beside us,
and you left me inside whilst you escaped,
we didn't realise that the game we played,
would scar us both for eternity.

*where did it all go wrong?*

### sour end
you painted the truth with the sweetest lies. and i kept my eyes dry whenever i needed to cry. you gave me plasters for the internal bleeding. i wish i knew the blank pages you were reading. you fed me fallacies but starved me of reality. the sour end caused all these cavities. now my reflection is missing in the mirror. and the water falling from my eyes isn't getting any clearer. my heart is sinking in an ocean i created. lost in a place that's extremely gated. will i ever find silence in a mind that doesn't forget our memories? or will i find violence remembering my hero became my enemy?

*where did it all go wrong?*

i was hopelessly in love with you,
i wish you warned me,
that it wasn't worth,
falling in love with a demon.

*where did it all go wrong?*

my favourite poems,
were about you,
but now they mean nothing,
because you don't exist,
between these lines anymore.

*where did it all go wrong?*

### *strangers*
i know we're strangers but at least i know myself now. i didn't understand the danger until i saw it for myself now. we were once inseparable until we separated. you were forever present until the room was vacated. a heart filled with trust and warmth until it became cold. we peaked whilst we were young so our love didn't grow old. i knew your favourite places and the things you hated. i knew all your faces except for when you're feeling migrated. every detail was etched into my heart until it vanished. and i had access to the key until i was banished. i guess your love was peeling underneath and covered in gloss. now that you're gone, i'm sorry for your loss.

*where did it all go wrong?*

you brought out the best in me,
now i only see the worst in me,
i miss the person i was around you.

*where did it all go wrong?*

**interest**
when did you lose interest? was it before you laid my heart to rest? did you forget the memories we made? i could never forget you're the reason my soul was saved. did you forget all our dates and getaways? did you lose interest in our lazy days? did the feelings fade in your smile and laughter? was i just blind to the impending disaster? did you lose interest because you found better things? or did you become bored from everything? was i just a spur of the moment? or something you clung onto at your lowest? it's fine that you lost interest, i know better for next time. i just hope there isn't a next time.

*where did it all go wrong?*

you told me it's you and not me,
but it feels like i've done wrong,
even though it's your feelings that changed.

*where did it all go wrong?*

i wish you cared a little more,
about letting me down gently,
instead of letting everything,
crash and burn.

*where did it all go wrong?*

### *infatuation*
was our love just infatuated addiction? was our love just a contradiction? it was toxic but we were happy to fuel the flames. we were happy to verbally bring each other shame. maintaining this love was the hardest mission. because i tried to make amends but you wouldn't listen. we needed real love, not fake laughs. we needed the right way, not the wrong path.

*where did it all go wrong?*

tell me, will i ever get over you?
tell me, will this pain subside?
tell me, will someone else take your place?
tell me, was i a fool for loving you?
tell me, was i just a mistake?
tell me, was the love really real?
tell me, will i end up forgetting you?
tell me, will i ever find a love that's real?
tell me, will i ever trust again?

*where did it all go wrong?*

with all this pain,
the colour has left my face,
with all this rain,
i feel so out of place,
now i hope i never see your face again,
and never end up in the same place again.

*where did it all go wrong?*

we weren't made for each other,
we were just trials for each other,
tests and lessons for us to overcome,
in the end, we were made for other people.

*where did it all go wrong?*

**dreamworld**
i'm collecting every piece of my heart and discarding it away. counting all of the wasted days. picking and burning all of the baggage. in the hopes that it will lessen the damage. i'm starting over, rebuilding myself for the next person. but until then i'll have to close the curtains. i'm afraid of letting someone else in to repeat our story. because when i look back at what you did, it feels so gory. it's hard to mourn someone that's still living. because you know that everything, they've done feels unforgiving. you'll do everything you can to avoid them in the real world. but you'll continue reuniting with them in every dream world.

*where did it all go wrong?*

i never should have relied on you so much,
maybe that's why it was too much,
because i became too much,
and you became suffocated by love,
and you decided you had enough.

*where did it all go wrong?*

when i look into the mirror,
i still see what we once were,
i look into my eyes,
and i see how much i miss,
your touch and your love,
your smile and your face,
your hair and your hugs,
and then i see the pain and hurt,
all over again.

*where did it all go wrong?*

now that there's no more you,
i have to let go,
but i can't let it go,
because there's no more you.

*where did it all go wrong?*

### *maybe*
maybe i'm just kidding myself. but these thoughts are of no help. i'm wondering maybe you might just come back. maybe we might just get our journey back on track. but i've accepted, that you were not someone i deserved. i just didn't do enough to stop everything being burned. if i changed, would you return? or is this a sign that i never learn? i've taken the blame because it's easier than pointing fingers. especially when our opinions constantly differ. one day maybe we can revisit this with a laugh and a hug. and agree that our temporary time together was enough.

*where did it all go wrong?*

the idea of a happy couple,
and a perfect life,
was simply a fairy tale,
that was too good,
to be true.

*where did it all go wrong?*

### *heartless*
after you, i was heartless, because i never experienced heart ache. you left with my heart so i didn't experience heartbreak. it was far worse because i was without a heart. i had to construct a new heart to restart. relearning the emotions, you stole. building a new shield to protect my soul. treating every visitor in my life with the utmost kindness. because despite all the pain, i unlocked a new kind of brightness. there's a glow to my smile and a mercy in my eyes. it feels like no one else can hurt me with anymore lies. i feel like i can grow gracefully old. because i went from being heartless to a heart full of gold.

*where did it all go wrong?*

i was at my lowest after you,
i'm grateful for the experience,
even though it hurt a lot,
i grew despite all the pain.

*where did it all go wrong?*

you're the reason,
i don't believe in soulmates,
anymore.

*where did it all go wrong?*

i was a fool for loving you,
more than i loved myself,
i should have been selfish,
but i can't help this,
it's in my heart to be selfless.

*where did it all go wrong?*

**smile**
i don't smile anymore, because my heart is laid out on the floor. the windows are open and the doors are broken. it never stops aching. now i can't stop my heart from hating. you destroyed the home in my heart after building the walls. you planted all the seeds just to watch me fall. i was a fool for thinking we would last. because the time we spent together went by so fast. luckily, i don't miss you anymore. because i finally won the war inside my head. even if i'm surrounded by debris, i can't sleep peacefully in my bed.

*where did it all go wrong?*

i'm glad we don't speak now,
silence is better,
than reliving your voice.

*where did it all go wrong?*

i loved you when you were,
at your lowest,
so why couldn't you,
do the same for me?

*where did it all go wrong?*

maybe i should have hurt you,
the way you hurt me,
but fortunately for you,
i was raised to be kind.

*where did it all go wrong?*

i gave you my smile,
and the time that came with it,
and now it's been gone for a while,
i guess all these flowers,
only kept you smiling for so long,
and then the hours ran out,
i just wish i knew,
where did it all go wrong?

*where did it all go wrong?*

**anniversary**
today would have been our anniversary. but our relationship needed critical surgery. we missed out on the operations and fell apart. we broke each other's hearts. mine felt permanent and it will never heal. so on this day, i remember how everything used to feel. on this day, we should have been celebrating our love. but i don't blame you for finally having enough. on our broken anniversary, do you still think of me? or did that ship sink instantly? this day reminds me of your hairs draped down your shoulders. and the flowers i gathered to celebrate our love growing older. but just like the petals i would give you, our love shrivelled up and disappeared. and even now my heart cheers for you, despite that heartbreak interfered. so i hope you're spending this day doing something better. and maybe one day you'll read this letter.

*where did it all go wrong?*

it was a pleasure to experience,
this short-lived adventure with you,
and maybe one day we'll revisit it,
but for now, i hope we can be happier,
without each other.

*where did it all go wrong?*

when life fell apart,
you were there,
to pick me back up,
but now that you're gone,
life fell apart all over again.

*where did it all go wrong?*

will the clouds stop reminding me,
that you made my world so dark?
will the rain stop reminding me,
that i need to carry on crying over you?

*where did it all go wrong?*

**over you**
i'm finally over you, i don't need your love. thanks to you, i know that for me real love is more than enough. your version of love was conditional and twisted. i'm so lucky that our connection temporarily existed. now i've found a love that obsesses over one another. you could have had it all but you made me suffer. now that i'm over you, i've found a love that heals my soul. i found a love that doesn't leave me with holes. you lost a love that would have been unconditional. so now if i see you again, i'll act like you're invisible.

*where did it all go wrong?*

give me reasons,
for why i should forgive you,
give me reasons,
for why i should forget you,
give me reasons,
for why i should take the blame,
give me reasons,
for why i shouldn't hate you.

*where did it all go wrong?*

what scares me the most,
is that if you could break my heart,
what's stopping someone else,
from doing it all over again?

*where did it all go wrong?*

things never turn out,
the way you planned them,
that's why we didn't meet,
any of our expectations.

*where did it all go wrong?*

**a forever love**
i guess i wanted the type of love where we grow old together. but you preferred living in the moment instead of living in forever. i planted seeds so that we could grow. i tried to be your sunshine so you could glow. but you washed away the hard work. and you threw salt into the dirt. smashing every bulb you could find so darkness could take over. and eventually you pushed me away when i tried to get closer. we both wanted different types of love. maybe something everlasting was too much. because you wanted short and sweet. and i wanted a love where i'd feel complete.

*where did it all go wrong?*

now that you're gone,
i don't have to spend anymore,
of my love on you.

*where did it all go wrong?*

i wish i could go back,
to never meeting you,
i would have avoided you,
and if i still stumbled into your path,
i'd run the other way,
just so i could survive.

*where did it all go wrong?*

i'm lucky,
that you're no longer,
ruining my life.

*where did it all go wrong?*

### never go back
let's agree to never go back to what we used to be. because i know i never want to revisit that side of me. you hurt me but without you i grew so much more. my life finally began when i shut the door. i might not trust anyone with my heart but i know not to hurt them the way you hurt me. and i know you don't deserve whoever you find, the way you didn't deserve me. let's agree to remove these memories of us. because i don't want to remember anything to do with us.

*where did it all go wrong?*

i can't fall in love,
anymore,
until i love myself.

*where did it all go wrong?*

one day i'll find someone,
someone who loves me,
despite all my flaws,
someone who love me,
despite how many times i fall,
one day i'll find someone,
who matches my soul,
someone who loves me,
the way i love them.

*where did it all go wrong?*

### *farewell*
i'm sorry i wasn't perfect. but i didn't deserve it. i didn't deserve the betrayal and the solitude. or the chaos that ensued. you broke me down and scattered all the pieces. turning my life into a puzzle where the struggle never ceases. i escaped a jungle of avalanches. and that wasn't without you snapping all the branches. i learnt how to love myself without having to love you. i'm able to smile knowing i only ever loved you. i did my bit but you didn't do yours. so on your way out i permanently closed the door. now when you reappear in my mind, i'm able to think of you calmly. so i'm okay now because this goodbye was our finale.

*where did it all go wrong?*

for the rest of my life,
i'll be asking myself,
where did it all go wrong?

Printed in Great Britain
by Amazon